YOU KNOW YOU ARE

AN ENGINEER...

by Richard McChesney

illustrated by Woolly

You Know You Are An Engineer... celebrates the quirky characteristics that are universally understood by anyone who knows or lives with an engineer, or technically minded person.

This is the third book in the "You Know You Are" book series, and was assembled with help from engineers, their families and colleagues.

Other books in the "You Know You Are" series are:

- You Know You Are A Runner...
- You Know You Are A Nurse...
- You Know You Are A Dog Lover...
- You Know You Are A Golfer...
- You Know You Are Getting Older...
- You Know You Are A Teacher...
- You Know You Are A Mother...

Visit www.YouKnowYouAreBooks.com to join our mailing list and be notified when future titles are released, or find us at www.facebook.com/YouKnowYouAreBooks, or follow us on twitter (@YouKnowYouAreBK)

You Know You Are An Engineer...

First edition published 2013 by Strictly Business Limited

Happy reading!

YOU KNOW YOU ARE AN ENGINEER
WHEN, IN COLLEGE, YOU THOUGHT SPRING
BREAK WAS A METAL FATIGUE FAILURE...

YOU KNOW YOU ARE AN ENGINEER
WHEN RATHER THAN BUY A TV, YOU SPENT
THREE TIMES AS MUCH ON PARTS AND
BUILT IT FROM THE GROUND UP...

YOU KNOW YOU ARE AN ENGINEER
WHEN THE FIRST THING YOU DO WITH
ANYTHING NEW IS PULL IT APART TO
SEE HOW IT WORKS...

YOU KNOW YOU ARE AN ENGINEER
WHEN THE ONLY PEOPLE WHO LAUGH
AT YOUR JOKES ARE THOSE WHO
TOOK CLASSES IN MULTIVARIATE
CALCULUS AND PARTICLE PHYSICS...

YOU KNOW YOU ARE AN ENGINEER

WHEN PRIOR TO BUYING YOUR FIANCEE
HER ENGAGEMENT RING, YOU CALCULATED
THE CORRECT RING SIZE BY SECRETLY
MEASURING HER RING FINGER WITH A
SET OF CALLIPERS...

YOU KNOW YOU ARE AN ENGINEER
WHEN THAT 4 YEAR DEGREE WAS THE
BEST 6 YEARS OF YOUR LIFE...

YOU KNOW YOU ARE AN ENGINEER
WHEN YOU CAN'T HELP EAVESDROPPING
IN COMPUTER STORES...AND CORRECTING
THE SALESPERSON...

YOU KNOW YOU ARE AN ENGINEER
WHEN YOU HAVE A NEATLY SORTED
COLLECTION OF OLD BOLTS AND
NUTS IN YOUR GARAGE...

YOU KNOW YOU ARE AN ENGINEER
WHEN YOU GO ON A CRUISE AND ASK FOR A
PERSONAL TOUR OF THE ENGINE ROOM...

YOU KNOW YOU ARE AN ENGINEER
WHEN YOU CONSIDER YOURSELF WELL
DRESSED IF YOUR SOCKS MATCH...

YOU KNOW YOU ARE AN ENGINEER

WHEN YOUR WIFE DOESN'T HAVE A CLUE
AS TO WHAT YOU DO AT WORK...

YOU KNOW YOU ARE AN ENGINEER
WHEN YOU HAVE NO LIFE AND YOU CAN PROVE IT MATHEMATICALLY...

YOU KNOW YOU ARE AN ENGINEER
WHEN YOU HAVE MODIFIED YOUR CAN
OPENER TO BE MICROPROCESSOR DRIVEN...

YOU KNOW YOU ARE AN ENGINEER
WHEN YOU HAVE ADDED AN ELECTRIC
MOTOR TO YOUR EXERCISE BIKE...

YOU KNOW YOU ARE AN ENGINEER
WHEN YOU KNOW THE 2ND LAW OF
THERMODYNAMICS BUT NOT YOUR SHIRT SIZE...

YOU KNOW YOU ARE AN ENGINEER
WHEN YOU KNOW THAT TIME TRAVEL IS IMPOSSIBLE BUT YOU HAVE DESIGNED YOUR OWN TIME MACHINE...

YOU KNOW YOU ARE AN ENGINEER
WHEN YOU KNOW EXACTLY HOW MANY
STEPS THERE ARE IN EACH SET OF
STAIRS AT THE OFFICE...

1st Floor 6 Steps

2nd Floor 7 Steps

3rd Floor 5 Steps

YOU KNOW YOU ARE AN ENGINEER

WHEN YOU HAVE TROUBLE JUSTIFYING
BUYING FLOWERS FOR YOUR GIRLFRIEND
INSTEAD OF SPENDING THE MONEY TO
UPGRADE YOUR COMPUTERS RAM...

YOU KNOW YOU ARE AN ENGINEER

WHEN YOU LOAD THE DISHWASHER TO
MAXIMIZE THE PACKING EFFICIENCY...

YOU KNOW YOU ARE AN ENGINEER
WHEN YOU LIKE REPAIRING THINGS
MORE THAN ACTUALLY USING THEM...

YOU KNOW YOU ARE AN ENGINEER
WHEN YOU LAUGH AT JOKES
ABOUT MATHEMATICIANS...

YOU KNOW YOU ARE AN ENGINEER
WHEN YOU KNOW WHICH DIRECTION THE WATER SWIRLS WHEN YOU FLUSH...

YOU KNOW YOU ARE AN ENGINEER
WHEN YOU THINK YOUR COMPUTER
LOOKS BETTER WITHOUT THE COVER...

YOU KNOW YOU ARE AN ENGINEER
WHEN YOU THINK THAT WHEN PEOPLE
YOU'RE TALKING TO YAWN, IT'S BECAUSE
THEY HAVEN'T HAD ENOUGH SLEEP...

YOU KNOW YOU ARE AN ENGINEER
WHEN YOU STILL OWN A SLIDE RULE
AND YOU KNOW HOW TO USE IT...

YOU KNOW YOU ARE AN ENGINEER

WHEN YOU LOOK FORWARD TO CHRISTMAS BECAUSE YOU WILL GET TO ASSEMBLE THE KIDS TOYS...

YOU KNOW YOU ARE AN ENGINEER
WHEN YOUR FAVORITE ACTOR IS R2D2...

MOVIE PREMIERE

YOU KNOW YOU ARE AN ENGINEER
WHEN YOU USE A CAD PACKAGE AND
A WIND TUNNEL TO DESIGN AND TEST
YOUR SON'S DERBY CAR...

YOU KNOW YOU ARE AN ENGINEER
WHEN YOU THOUGHT THE REAL
HEROES OF APOLLO 13 WERE
THE MISSION CONTROLLERS...

YOU KNOW YOU ARE AN ENGINEER
WHEN YOU HAVE TAKEN THE BACK OFF
YOUR TV JUST TO SEE WHATS INSIDE...

YOU KNOW YOU ARE AN ENGINEER

WHEN YOUR WIFE ALWAYS ASKS FOR THE "SHORT VERSION" WHEN SHE ASKS HOW SOMETHING WORKS...

YOU KNOW YOU ARE AN ENGINEER
WHEN YOUR THREE YEAR OLD SON ASKS WHY
THE SKY IS BLUE AND YOU TRY TO EXPLAIN
ATMOSPHERIC ABSORPTION THEORY...

YOU KNOW YOU ARE AN ENGINEER
WHEN YOUR I.Q. IS HIGHER
THAN YOUR WEIGHT...

YOU KNOW YOU ARE AN ENGINEER
WHEN YOU'RE NEVER WRONG AND CAN BACK IT UP WITH FACTS...

YOU KNOW YOU ARE AN ENGINEER
WHEN YOU ARE CURRENTLY GATHERING
THE COMPONENTS TO BUILD YOUR
OWN NUCLEAR REACTOR...

So... are you an
Engineer?

You have just read the third book in the "You Know You Are" series.

Other "You Know You Are" books are:

- You Know You Are A Runner...
- You Know You Are A Nurse...
- You Know You Are A Dog Lover...
- You Know You Are A Golfer...
- You Know You Are Getting Older...
- You Know You Are A Teacher...
- You Know You Are A Mother...

If you enjoyed this book why not join our mailing list to be notified when future titles are released – visit www.YouKnowYouAreBooks.com, or find us on facebook (www.facebook.com/YouKnowYouAreBooks), or follow us on twitter (@YouKnowYouAreBK)